MARTIN DICKINSON

I AM THAT ROAD

Beltway EDITIONS

MARTIN DICKINSON

I AM THAT ROAD

NEW AND SELECTED POEMS

Beltway
EDITIONS

Published by Beltway Editions, 4810 Mercury Drive, Rockville, Maryland 20853.

www.beltwayeditions.com

Printed in the United States of America
10 9 8 7 6 5 4 3 2 1

Book Design: Jorge Ureta Sandoval
Cover photo: Dorothea Lange, *U.S. No. 54 North of El Paso Texas. One of the westward routes of the migrants, 1938*. Library of Congress, Prints and Photographs Division.
ISBN: 978-1-957372-19-8

Beltway Editions (www.beltwayeditions.com)
4810 Mercury Drive
Rockville, MD 20853
Indran Amirthanayagam: Publisher
Sara Cahill Marron: Publisher

For Nancy

Contents

The fight is won or lost far away from witnesses –
behind the lines, in the gym, and out there on the road,
long before I dance under those lights.

Muhammad Ali, (Interview)

O public road, I say back I am not afraid to leave you,
yet I love you, you express me better than I can express myself.

Walt Whitman, "Song of the Open Road"

Antes de recorrer mi camino yo era mi camino.

Before I travelled my road I was my road.

Antonio Porchia, *Voces*

MARTIN DICKINSON

I AM THAT ROAD

NEW AND SELECTED POEMS

I. ROAD

Of My Birth

He not busy being born is busy dying.
Bob Dylan, "It's Alright, Ma (I'm only bleeding)"

Of my birth I know nothing,
but this photo
Albany Airport, 1949.

Passengers in gray coats,
nervous, huddled in the cold,
scarves, hair blowing

in January wind, gaze
to the looming DC-3.
Checkerboard-painted water tower

juts upward behind
an ominous wing. For many
their first flight ever.

My aunt, labor and delivery nurse,
rests an elbow on the chain link fence,
awaits her passage through clouds

to a sister's side in a faraway city
as the aircraft draws closer,
the word *Columbus* painted

in big letters on its fuselage. Nothing
but the granular truth presents itself.
Propeller blades splice winter air

frozen in photographic time.
The plane taxis toward the little group
by the rusted sign that reads

Gate 2 as the gate swings
open to her first voyage.
Wide open.

Apologia Pro Vita Sua

Born of it and borne by it,
fire, fire of the iron city.
From the top bunk, awake,
my gaze across to the slag dump,
the surface of a molten planet,
nighttime aflame, ashen,
ore of my body, metallurgy
of my eyes steeled in the steel city,
hammered by it. The liturgy of it
begins my life. Incense,
but acrid. From my window
above the railway cut
endless trains, rusty.

Slag trains, molten refuse.
Limestone, coal, iron,
sixty percent of America's
self in pursuit of its steel self,
highways, bridges, train tracks,
boxcars, boxcars, boxcars.
I, born of it and borne by it,
of fire, of slag, of schlock,
my child's innocent gaze
on the ceaseless red-hot dumping
of the huge slag buckets.
It's me, it's me, the fire still inside
the iron still inside, the rust.

Jimi Hendrix

Or bid the soul of Orpheus sing such notes
As warbled to the string, Drew iron tears
down Pluto's cheek.
John Milton, *"Il Penseroso"*

The dream, the illusion,
those riffs and wah-wahs.
You are pure illusion,
a flare-up of light in whom
we believed in that moment.

Baltimore, the pavilion, wet lawn.
sharp raindrops fall around us,
hail, lightning. Zeus speaks
as you sing your thunder
in that Olympus moment.

Too soon you are gone.
I miss the thunder, the rain,
sounds that never
existed before or since.
Where did you go?

We are drenched
by a downpour of sound,
a haze of purple.

Editing the War

Vietnam, your latest game you're playing with your blackest queen.
Donovan Leitch, "Ballad of a Crystal Man"

What do I not talk about?
Not talk about the defoliated trees?
the maelstrom of lies,
shrapnel wounds of children,
unexploded ordnance years after,
not my arrest at the Pentagon,
the smell of urine in the cell?

Not about when we held hands to pray
for victims, napalm-burnt flesh?
Not phony body count stories,
copters whirring overhead,
the loss, the loss, the loss?
Friends come home
arms in slings, bloody wound of a nation
stinging odor of tear gas in streets?

What not to talk about? Do I mention
these names, edit out mothers' tears
those who stand next to me now,
their Capitol reflected in black marble?
My finger traces one name,
then another, another, another.

Coffee, Beaujolais, Marlboros

For Julia Cameron

Coffee, Beaujolais,
Marlboros, Browning,
your face framed, blonde hair,
coffee, Beaujolais.
Curled smoke of evening,
poetry of the moment
in those days, coffee,
Marlboros, more Robert Browning,
sun subsided as we wandered
across the Potomac bridge.

My sun sets to rise again
Days of travel on foot,
reciting scribbled notebook poetry,
sandwich suppers, luscious
smoke rising from joints.

Shared a little Ginsberg,
"Wichita Vortex Sutra"
Planet News first edition
(still have it, worn, yellowed),
American Eagle beating its wings over Asia,
ash in the coffee cup, Dylan.
Beaujolais, Marlboros, coffee.

In the bookstore now
I thumb your book. Yes.
The Artist's Way.

I sit to consume it cover-to-cover.
Yes, the way, the path,
via dell'arte. You were right.
Ginsberg was right,
Browning was right,
My sun sets to rise again.

Wisconsin Newspaper Strike

Fourteen below at sunrise,
chain link fence,
our boots crunch snow.
Bright sun, wind,
along the highway shoulder.

Purification of ice, of cold,
purification of purpose.
How many mornings, how many days?
We are conga-line close.
Numb fingers clutch picket signs.

I give a car hood a shove,
another one a shove,
a bang with my picket sign.
Car exhaust at fourteen below,
smoke from oil drum fire.

Are losing and winning the same?
Brutal, brutal Wisconsin,
odor of stale thermos coffee,
fingers numb, snow.
How many mornings?

I Am That Road

All the roads I have taken
come together, leaves falling
blowing across the highway
or that baking hot road in Indiana
that time in a previous life.

I see now Whitman's open road
flag of America, stars in a blue field,
narrow stripes stretched out
like roads, all the roads I've taken.
Fixing a flat in Wisconsin snow,
pavement icy, hands frozen
pumping up my Volkswagen,
up and up with the cold metal jack.

My foot on the pedal
across the bridge to Winona, Minnesota,
Mississippi flows below me
thick with floating ice.
I go and come now still via many roads
through tunnels, past toll booths,
rail crossings with Ginsberg's boxcars,
gate up, the flashing light stops
so I can go onward. Stop and go,
fast and slow, all the roads I've taken
become me, and I am that road.

Homage to Euclid

What has been affirmed without proof can also be denied without proof.
Euclid, *Euclid's Elements*

What points are these,
visible to us, yet revealing something invisible,
invisible, yet real?

What lines that reach beyond the page?
Here's a music of objects: rhomboid, oblong,
parallelogram,

a rhapsody of postulates with space enough
for basilicas, grids for towns, all to be filled in
later.

Here's the circle, here the sphere
and all that white space to surround them.
Here's room enough for worlds.

Fortune Cookie Man

Here inside where I sit everything glows,
paper and pencils spread across tabletops.

Wealth and prosperity are in your future,
you know. This is my poetry.

When it is dark outside, do not complain:
open your mind to the stars.

The fortunes I write shine in the dark.
Wisdom comes from experience.

Your own deeds speak so much louder
than another's words.

Ask me how I can see your present and future.
Simple, they are my present, my future.

Even though you do not know me,
I know you—better than you might think.

Writings are my deeds, the only things
I truly long for now.

Once I had a lover, but she disappeared.
Everything eventually disappears.

To love and be loved is like
feeling the sun from both sides.

Allow confidence
to carry you through each day.

Cape Cod Coyote

Scraggy apparition, who am I to question why you're here,
brown, black and silver against morning light?

Why shouldn't you squat in beach grass to leave your scat,
watch the sun peek over the headlands,

or take a dip in the bay same as any creature? What does it have to do
with my walk to see the sunrise?

Clouds scud above the surface as the water glistens
with first rays of bright,

almost as good as one of those paintings in the art galleries
on Commercial Street in town,

but you wouldn't make it into one of those: forelegs covered
with sand, mangy hock and hind legs.

Must've swum the canal, you or those ancestors of yours,
or maybe trotted over the bridge in broad day.

I'm the visitor, so lope off as if you own this beach. Just you and me
out here, buddy: you, me and the terns.

Teotihuacan

For Beatriz Valencia Ochoa

O the two-thousand-year dust,
sun baked stones,

stones of time in its stillness,
blood-stained time,

roadway of the dead,
carved birds on patio pillars.

The pyramid of the sun
yearns toward a cloudless sky.

City of gods, of the obsidian knife
of death.

O to die here and be reborn, to fly
like a sacred butterfly upward,

upward into that sun.

Fortune

For Salgado Maranhão

Chance, luck, a cause
of changes in one's affairs,
roll of the dice,
genetic disposition.

A ladder, a burning emblem,
the spot where the apple lands
dropped from its branch.
Caprice.

Often personified as a goddess,
thought to distribute lots
according to whim.
What's my whim?

Her symbol the wheel
of vicissitude,
of happenstance,
of fire.

My fortune is to be.
To be what?

To be.

Shaker Round Barn

The hayings come and gone,
the great mow empty
yet still a fortress,
still the circular stone pattern,
still the orderly row
of milking stalls
ready for cattle
that never come,
or the majestic loft
for children to jump from
into an imaginary hay pile,
into the stale odor

of oblivion.
Castle of a gone world
of invisible workmen
who shape a utopia
out of nowhere,
lay limestone
under the sun's orbit,
Where are they
who came before us,
their rotunda stable
empty now,
empty and waiting?

Western Avenue

Side of the diamond
of my designed city,
line of demarcation,
from my window,
night headlights reflect
in your asphalt.
I salute your
traffic lights that glow
red, yellow, green.
From my city, my capital,
I overlook an adjoining state.
You are a horizon,
a line of perspective,
elm-arced,
to remind me that all my life
I have crossed boundaries
just as I will go back and forth
over you again and again
in my zigzag future.

Western Avenue, red taillights
reach along you in search of their destinies.
You mark a world,
a geography, an edge
of jurisdictions,
the brick sidewalk
of your Maryland half
where pedestrians amble
under copper streetlights.
All my life I have sought

crisp and defined things
only to watch
certainty melt away,
but you are sharp, definite.
Western Avenue, I embrace you,
a line dropped onto a chart
by our forebears
leading northeastward
to the vanishing point.

Alberto Fino, Cement Mason (1960 – 2008)

En el último instante, toda mi vida durará un instante.
In the final instant, my whole life will last an instant.
Antonio Porchia, *Voces*

Ash, limestone, gravel,
a swirling mix, shaper
of the world. The art
of this, beat and pound
of the job. From my safe street
I see. I see it all.

They hoist you in a bright red sling,
a basket stretcher craned above
the huge hole. Clay, empty space,
your body against the sky,
above where they pushed
on your rib cage till a pulse returned.

Caught in the act of doing
what you really do, pour
the soupy gray mass into
big blue buckets, torso
caked in fine white dust.
One step wrong, Alberto,
and you tumble 30 feet down,
scaffolding collapsing on you.

Adiós, inmigrante,
adios, trabajador,

constructor de mundos,
adios albañil.

The paper says you died
in the emergency room.
Ash, limestone, gravel,
a swirling mix, O shaper
of the world. Blue helmets
will descend again
into the hole. Work will pulse.
The art of this, the beat and pound.
A building will rise.

From my safe street
I see. I see it all.

La poesía nos hace tocar lo impalpable y escuchar
la marea del silencio cubriendo un paisaje devastado
por el insomnio.

Octavio Paz, *La llama doble*,

Poetry enables us to touch the impalpable and to hear the tide of silence that covers a landscape devastated by insomnia.

Octavio Paz, *The Double Flame*

Bienvenido, inmigrante

Cada paso que damos en la tierra nos lleva
a un mundo nuevo . . .
Federico García Lorca

Bienvenido al desierto de cardos, a las montañas anaranjadas,
arroyos secos, torres de vigilancia y a tu nuevo país,

a la tierra prometida, tierra de los sueños,
de una nueva bandera.

En la tierra prometida que no promete nada, donde los sueños
pueden ser pesadillas.

Bienvenido con tu mochila, zapatillas gastadas, botella de
agua, esperanza.

Bienvenido a carreteras donde sale y se pone el sol, trozos de
neumáticos viejos al costado de la carretera,

a los depósitos de chatarra a las vías del tren, a todo lo que
puedas imaginar y más, la internet, la riqueza que no puede ser
para ti.

a la poesía de las noches en la ciudad, bailarines, llamas del
amor, graffiti y el olor a orina en el paso subterráneo,

todo al alcance y todo fuera de alcance
como la justicia, un trabajo en progreso.

Estarás cansado, tendrás sed. No te olvides de descansar.
No te olvides de beber el agua de la tristeza.

Welcome, Immigrant

Each step we take on earth carries us to a new world.
Federico García Lorca

Welcome to the desert of thistles, of orange mountains,
dry streams, watchtowers, and to your new country,

to the promised land, land of dreams,
of a new flag.

To the promised land that promises nothing and where dreams
may be nightmares.

Welcome with your backpack, worn out sneakers, water bottle,
and hope.

Welcome to highways where sun rises and sets, pieces
of old tires on the side of the road,

to junkyards, train tracks, to everything you can imagine
and more,
the internet, the wealth that may not be for you.

to the poetry of nights in the city, dancers, flames of love,
graffiti
and the smell of urine in the underpass,

to everything within reach and everything out of reach
like justice, a work in progress.

You will be tired, thirsty. Don't forget to rest.
Don't forget to drink the water of sadness.

Memoria

ahora y siempre
es nunca
Alejandra Pizarnik

Cada momento presente se vuelve pasado,
aroma de un limón que primero es cortado en rodajas,
mancha circular de taza de café en un mostrador.

Levanto almas de mis amados.
Levanto mi propia alma.
Cada momento pasado se vuelve presente.

Memoria

now and always
is never
Alejandra Pizarnik

Every present becomes past,
aroma of lemon first sliced open,
circular coffee cup stain on a counter.

I raise up souls of loved ones.
I raise up my own soul.
Every past becomes present.

Virgen del Tepeyac

Habrías visto las jacarandás
en flor púrpura en esta época del año,
Rascacielos de la Ciudad de México como agujas distantes
contra los lejanos picos del Ajusco
mucho más allá los tejados
de vuestras basílicas gemelas,
y visto hoy si estuvieras aquí hoy
quizás también la carretera torcida
de mi vida que condujo a tu cima,
por medio de la escalera de Jacob

de subir y descansar, subir y descansar,
a esta vista del altiplano que es
el centro de México, esa es tu casa
en un sentido, donde siempre has vivido
y visto no solo en la distancia
pero en el pasado, presente y futuro
como ahora llego a tu capilla para contemplar
este jardín, estas llamas
de buganvillas y de
rosas, sí, rosas milagrosas.

Virgin of Tepeyac

You would have seen the jacarandas
in purple bloom this time of year,
Mexico City skyscrapers distant needles
against far Ajusco peaks
above and beyond
rooftops of your twin basilicas,
and were you here, perhaps,
perhaps also the twisted highway
of my life leading to your hilltop,
by means of a Jacob's Ladder

of climb and rest, climb and rest,
to this vista of the altiplano,
central Mexico, your home
where you have always lived
and seen not just into distance
but into past, present, future
as now I reach your chapel,
this garden, these flames
of bougainvillea and of
roses, yes, the miracle roses.

II. TIME

Nostos

August, sixty-one years ago,
I stand at the screen door,
shade of the kitchen at my back,
morning smell of bacon crackling.
Conical poplars line the drive,
with its manicured strip of grass,
paved tire tracks. From the hood
of the blue '51 Packard, a chrome swan
leans forward ready to take flight.

I run my index finger along
the grid of screen. Jonquil Place:
home, always present. Deep green
elms arch over the little yard,
the rustle of their leaves, the whirr
and stop of a hand mower,
a streetcar that rattles along
on Pennsylvania Boulevard,
the thick summer air of that place.

Periodic Table

Too small to be perceived by the senses,
they are eternal and have many different shapes,
and they can cluster together to create
things that are perceivable.
Democritus, 430 B.C.

Onward they march
in their little boxes,
truncated groupings.
Hydrogen, Helium,
Lithium, Beryllium.
The gods get theirs:
Mercury, Neptune.
And Uranus: Uranium,
Pluto: Plutonium--
those genii we'd like
to put back in their lamps.
Then Einstein, Fermi
and Ernest Rutherford
get theirs, too—
all highly radioactive.
At last comes
Ununoctium,
a dab of colorless,
odorless (but noble) gas
lasting less than
one one-thousandth
of a second.

But then,
what's time anyway
to an element?

My Concept of Time

The March breeze shakes a leafless willow oak branch
up and down, up and down—that's it.
Duration in which an event happens: for the wasp
to chew wood pulp into its papier-maché nest,
for Orion to cross the sky. A ticking
that's neither wrong nor right.
My face in the mirror registers it,
surely, like a rhythm,
yet subtle, invisible, it may not
even exist at all
except as a way
of speaking,
a way of remaining
silent.

Portuguese Boats, Scituate Harbor

Deus quer, o homem sonha:
Fishermen, God wants,
man dreams. At night
you dreamt of the harvest
your nets would drag up,
fingers callused, bleeding,
the sting of salt, shining backs
of the codfish: *bacalhau*,
their flapping tailfins
slid down your ramps.
Pescadores, but now
you depart, blue mesh
nets hang ready,
the sky, too, ready.
Your journey is against
the orange sky, against
the green water.
Out past the light
the sea awaits you,
fluid and ethereal.
The earth seems solid,
but it is not so.
The tide does not stand still.
Once this whole earth
was one thing, a unified
and unseparated sea.
O reapers of the water,
you have known this
as over the dark waves
you cast forth your nets.

Sagrou-te e foste desvendando
a espuma: for He
made you holy,
revealing the foam,
and this is no dream.
Three hulls: *São Miguel,*
Silver Rose, Filomena,
you drift in the same fluid
as your prey, under the same
orange and glowing clouds.

Ninety-Six, Weymouth

Everything in this world leans against something
and so did you that birthday morning.
Wind coming off the bay, sun reflecting
on our windshield, we drove out to get
your new glasses because this world is worth seeing.
They fit perfectly. Coming home we passed
the naval air station long ago closed down,
the one for wars long since won, remembered
its empty hangars, big ones with their doors
wide open, waiting. Back at your place, one
aging man, one ancient, we stepped under
November branches that long since had dropped
their leaves. I felt gentle pressure of your leaning
on my arm: ninety-six-year-old pressure.

Enola Gay

One can step quietly past the silver machine
hung mid-air, admire the powerful wingspan

above all other warplanes in the Boeing hangar,
a mother eagle shielding her young, this fortress

named by the pilot for his mother, and can note
the meticulous care taken by her preservers,

the excruciating precision of her cockpit,
reflective surfaces gleaming and precise,

and one can know nothing about Little Boy,
that awful payload inserted into her bay

in the Tinian darkness, nothing at all of
the white roses nor the red roses burning

in the ruins, nor of the clocks stopped forever
in their towers at 8:15 a.m. Japan Time.

If I Should See a Single Bird

I would revel in its birdness,
focus intently on just that one bird
wings folded or outstretched,
for one bird is the whole world.
Yet it's this particular bird
as this world is this particular world,
and one bird itself becomes
a poem all by itself, as the poem
takes flight upward into a distance.
I'd recall a specific, particular
flock of Canada geese descending
precisely, particularly, into rushes
all in formation as though they were one
single bird, coming downward, downward
slanting in the same direction as
the sun's rays below a particular shining cloud.
And I would revel in the qualities
of that sunset or that poem
as if they were the whole world,
if I should see a single bird.

III. WINDSTORM

At Qasr Al-Yahud Baptism Site, West Bank

It's nothing like Verrochio's painting of it:
no dove descending, no haloed Jesus, no John the Baptist.

A burned-out army truck sinks into sand. Triangular
yellow signs, Arabic, Hebrew, English, warn of minefields.

Nothing like Verrochio's painting of it:
the path to the riverbank fenced in with barbed wire,

the world as it is, not as we might like it to be.
Spikey green bulrushes lean over the muddy stream

to touch a different world-- the Kingdom
of Jordan. Khaki soldiers take a cigarette break,

assault rifles resting beside them.
We carry plastic bottles to fill with the muddy water,

bottles to bring home: to another and far away
world. I dip a cupped hand and let water drip down

to the Jordan's surface. Desert sun
drenches us in heat. As she wades into the stream,

my friend from Michigan hands me
a phone to read her the baptismal vow's question

here in this world as it is, not,
as in Verrochio's painting, we might like it to be:

"Do you reject Satan,
all his works and all his empty promises?"

Fragile, Liquid, Hazardous or Perishable

Earth, air, water and fire for the Greeks
but these for the U.S. Postal Service
are the essential elements.
Should I confess brownies
(how perishable anyway?)
baked last night and neatly
tucked underneath the red soccer jersey?
And is the glass in the framed graduation
portrait not fragile? Always I cut the brown
paper bag and wrap the box tightly
within which these items are secreted.
Aftershave is liquid but I'm not telling
the new postal clerk,
the one with the honest face,
the one who makes eye contact,
though she asks her question
quickly so as to check her box
and move on.

I love the blue
uniforms with the eagle patch.
That stylized eagle with its massive
beak could rip open packages like mine
sent from a dutiful father to a son
in faraway Geneva, Switzerland and find
the calculus textbook which,
in wrong hands could be a hazard,
its learning used to fashion, say,

a nuclear weapon. The postal clerks
are all polite now, all customer friendly
and may not truly want to know.
And isn't the planet mostly liquid,
so what's a little aftershave more or less?
And isn't life fragile and hazardous?
And, come to think of it,
don't all things perish,
as the Greeks taught us?

What a Windstorm Teaches

That pieces of tile can break off a building,
fallen branches line sidewalks,
empty boxes slide
across the pavement

whether we want them to or not.
That there's nothing we can do
about traffic lights bouncing,
aluminum poles that snap.

Nothing to be done about
wires that don't connect
when wind rushes above the roof,
there being no invincible networks.

That chaos lies at the root of things
from unremembered time.
Of this the storm reminds us,
teaches, but do we learn?

Things invisible hover
as yet we cannot see. We feel
their effects, hidden causes,
surprises about to happen.

The gnarled maple comes down when we
least expect, root ball torn from the soil,
trunk across the roadway. We will not
be able to get where we are going.

Asleep

Afloat in your dream, you are a crescent
within the crescent of me,

my leg curled inside your leg,
ease of your breath,

how it comes and goes. My eyes
fix on the skin of your back,

curvature of a shoulder blade,
tiny blonde hairs

invisible at other times, the relaxation
of it,

us side by side, sheet resting on the slope
of your thigh,

you oblivious to my present thought,
to my hand, which cups

the inside of your upper arm, a place
where the softness is,

my chest as it expands and contracts
against your spine.

Strands of your hair entering my nostrils
with each inhalation, escape again

on the outbreath like the coming and going
of day and night.

Knife

Humbly you lie by my plate,
but you are not humble.
Stainless and pure,
but you are not pure.
Steel of Japan, you are not
Japanese. You rest, mirror of blade
reflecting ceiling lights,
at the ready.

My hand quivers
to hold you, O thing with soul
reincarnating ancestors:
sharpened stone of Neanderthal,
dagger, stiletto, poniard,
fixed bayonet, rusted Confederate knife
turned up from soil
by a Pennsylvania plough.

You yearn to hunt
the arctic seal, to wage battle,
to be thrust in a street fight
and to draw blood.
You have done evil,
and so you dream
of performing it
over and over again.

I grip your handle
sensing the dark truth.
We live, after all,

at knife-edge. Of that,
you are well aware. My palm
embraces you for a little while.
You will pass to other hands.
You will outlive me.

IV. LIST

Ars Poetica

To begin in the middle, end in the beginning
and arrive at the middle again, spend hour upon hour
alone emptying the mind of all thought,

hike out of breath along the mountains above
the rush of Conundrum Creek, or run your hand across
waving grass tops in the middle of a hayfield.

To ponder every limb, twig and leaf of the oak
outside your window, listen to the wind in the eaves at
midnight
and hear things that aren't there.

To fall passionately in love
with the same woman as a 14th Century Italian poet,
and then converse with the night sky.

To track the phases of the moon, and finally, cast
your ideas onto the waves without hope of them ever
returning:
this is poetry.

Dark Enough

For Stan Plumly

Verse, you'd say, was the turning.
When the ox turns at the furrow end
to start the next furrow. Black earth
came to mind hearing you say this,
callused hands on a plow scraping the soil.
The dark is dark enough now to talk about this.
It wouldn't have served to be laudatory.
And "laudatory," you'd have said, is a word
that should never be in a poem, nor should
words like "universe" or "cosmos."

Yes, you said that. The dark is dark enough now
to talk about this. We gathered at our table,
fluorescent lights humming above,
the dark outside, door propped open.
Summer crickets sang in the night. It wouldn't
have served the moment to be kind. Words
required a certain purity of being, each of us
alone in the silent pauses, each alone,
listening. And so tonight, emptiness, darkness.
Dark enough now to talk about this.

Sand Hills Beach

For my brother

None of the other beaches were like it,
gravel, mostly gravel, the rounded stones
smoothed by eons in the tide
clicking together like our glass marbles
back in the day, rolling under the froth
of each wave. And there it was, the visionary sky,
and the line of bay shoreline extending
to the distance on both sides. But you,
why were you there at all? This was not
the skyscraper in the financial district
looking out at Liberty with her torch.
I never figured out where in the cottage
you hid the alcohol, why you piled up
driftwood on the porch, the fireplace
never lit, nor the pan with days-old eggs
crusted to it. So why? To be next to the sky?
Somewhere there was a pier, yes, the town pier
where scallop boats came in, a pier aimed
perfectly toward the Atlantic horizon.
I never found out if it was gin or vodka,
never got a sense of whether
you'd ever used the charcoal grill out back.

In the dim past we wore each other's clothes.
They fit us perfectly. I could have been you.
One visit to the cottage we lounged
on the screened-in porch. Gulls cavorted
in the pond across Turner Road. They'd

slant in laughing, enjoying themselves
we supposed, then flapped their wings
to brake as their feet touched down
in the shallows. I asked if I could wear your
socks and underwear having forgotten to pack
enough hurrying for my plane. Yes, of course.
I never could figure out a lot of things,

the army green Jeep Wrangler
you never seemed to go anywhere in.
Yes, I might have been you, fallen
from grace, from the bank vice-president
suites with their lounge chairs, marble walls,
Manhattan views, ferries making way
from Staten Island to the Battery.
Back in the day we had the same football,
down to the school field where nobody
was around to play touch, ostensibly,
which always turned out to be tackle.

In the end you stopped taking my calls.
The voicemail got so full that all I heard were clicks.
None of the town beaches were like yours,
the high tide came up over the seawall
and left salt puddles in the road. The tide
of life, ebbing and flowing, coming and going.
The yes, the no, and the maybe,
the voicemail never taking up my greeting.
You would have liked to stay forever.
You just couldn't. I would have liked it, too,
always the one to want the impossible,
the one to save. You could have been me.

The times we waded along, our feet
in the gravel, the pain of that, but the cold bay
so numbing that soon we didn't feel it.
But we were alive. Yes, we were alive.

Life List Notes

Sandhill Cranes, trio in flight, Cherokee Marsh,
Madison, Wisconsin, May 15, 1978.

Whimbrel swooping over mudflat, Third Cliff,
Scituate, Massachusetts, September 8, 1982.

Yellow-Bellied Sapsucker, male,
Roosevelt Island, District of Columbia, May 5, 1984.

American Oystercatcher stalking beach
Okracoke Inlet, North Carolina, June 10, 1986.

Clark's Nutcracker darting among pine branches,
Mount Washburn, Yellowstone, Wyoming, August 22, 1991.

Snow Geese, flock of thousands, Chincoteague Inlet,
Assateague Island, Virginia, December 31, 1992.

Roseate Spoonbills, quartet roosting in mangrove,
Sanibel Island, Florida, March 30, 1995.

Peregrine Falcon wheeling over Precipice Trail,
Champlain Mountain, Maine, August 16, 2001.

Chimney Swift, fell down chimney, caught
and released, District of Columbia, June 2, 2012.

Putting Beowulf Back on the Shelf

The heft of it,
climbing the ladder
to reach the top shelf,
painters departed,
their paint-dripped cans,
rolled-up multicolor cloths.
Now to restore the library
to just-dried boards,
to grip the brown hardbound,
its title barely visible
on the threadbare spine.

Irresistible to open its cover,
my careful signature,
Martin H. Dickinson,
dated forty-five years,
January, 1972.
O, Beowulf,
once more you ship
with the spear Danes
above churning waves
toward the mead hall.
Once more you arm yourself.

You don the linked-ring garment,
brandish Hrunting, sacred sword.
You are empowered
by the boar's helmet.
Here are my faint pencil markings.
those of a twenty-year-old

where you stand at Grendel's pool
readying your fight,
the word horn encircled
where the poet signals
the coming fight.

Flod blode weol
The flood boils with blood
folk tosægon
the people look on
hatan heolfre.
the hot gore.
Horn stundum song
the horn at times sings
fuslic furðon leoð
also the death song.
Here the pencil glosses fade

once meant to remind me
of the battle horn's
summoning of warriors
What did I know then
of the ancient one,
Frederick Klaeber, toiling
at this very edition
under Berlin allied bombs,
notes and books having vanished
on the funeral pyre of history,
the text painstakingly reconstructed

line by line for this volume?
O proud warrior, return now

in the aroma of fresh paint,
to your space between
A History of the English Language
and *The Anglo-Saxon Dictionary.*
What did I know then
of the demons that lurk
in hot pools of sorrow?
What did I know then
of the dragons of the heart?

Healings

When the pines talk to one another,
When no moon would tell my secret . . .
Joan Aleshire, "Healing"

How they do it in Kildare
is dip a piece of rag into St. Brigid's well, cloth
cut from the garment of the ill one.

They tie it to the rag tree, an ash,
to let flap in the breeze, to let rot with time,
and so the illness wears away,

time itself (as well as St. Brigid)
being the healer. The pines will surround it
in silence.

The gibbous moon will pass overhead.
Things stored once indelibly in the mind we'll forget.
The ash tree will come in leaf,

the ash tree will go out of leaf.
The moon will grow old only to become young again.
It, too, will talk to the pines.

Brigid knew all this
when she found this well and asked
a Kildarian digger to round it out,

knew the ash tree
would go out of leaf and the ash tree
would come into leaf,

that a rag tied to the tree
would flutter away to nothing in the wind.
And so it is with all our healings.

At Swift's Grave

Nice brass plaque
they gave you, gothic nave
arced overhead.
Please know,
I'll never look at a horse
the same way.
You've sailed
beyond all savage indignation,
O crafty one, thus
I hesitate to tell you
about today's Yahoos, the lengths
to which they go,
warming the planet,
causing seas to rise, and then
the immodesty of
weapons in so many
hands, beyond what even you
might imagine,
you, who knew well
that the ridiculous,
beyond all possible irony,
could become the real.

Gallagh Man, National Museum of Ireland

Swallowed by the bog,
he dreamt the world
to the slow time of sphagnum,
curled to one side,

arms folded as though
in satisfaction with it,
his deerskin cape and all.
Through anaerobic ages

lying defiant in the lush
organic matter pressing
always down, down.
Mayo's lakes and mountains

morphed to strange shapes.
In sleep he created kingdoms
and after caused their downfall,
all the while keeping secrets,

ever patient beneath
the footsoles of his conquerors,
conquerors who, themselves,
were conquered.

Mirrors of Venice

In the floral bordered one
with blossom-shaped gobs of crystal
I am in a glass wonderland,
burnt orange, crimson globes,
stretched-out sapphire drop vases.
The old Venetians laugh,
their mirrors still here to watch us.
In the 18th Century mirror,
its silver badly tarnished,
pockmarked, I am surrounded
by a murky, smoky world.
In the paired stairwell mirrors
hundreds of me extend to infinity,
each dimmer than the me before.
The very city they have left us
is a mirror. It is all about looking.
Bulbous palazzi surround me
in the convex shop window mirror.
And it is all about seeing: to see,
to be seen and be doubly seen.
In another shop window mirrored
red and blue motorboats tied up
at the canal's edge rock on waves
hardly visible. And it is about water,
this place that stands always against
that greatest of mirrors to the sky,
water, that turquoise gem,
yes, even in the gray of January.

Minor White, *Vicinity of Dansville, New York, 1955*

For some reason there are two barns,
the big one and the little one,
accompanying each other against a dark sky.
The clouds above ridged like ocean waves
for some reason mirror the rows of alfalfa
in the field, an ominous telephone pole shadow
cast across it, a line of demarcation within
the black space behind the two barns.
For some reason there is a clarity to black
and white that shows the world truly,
shows it to be this way and no other.
Such truths, for some reason, are hard to take,
the tough basics, the stark reality.
Art is truth that may not be beautiful.
Once we grasp a thing, it creates an awe
and a reverence in us. Could the sky be angry
because of what lives around or inside us?
Could the clouds be clouds of negativity,
charged particles, dark matter peeking
at us from behind those two neat barns
arrayed at a perfect right angle to each other
along the black horizon? Oh yes, the horizon.
That telephone pole casts its shadow,
an arm of doom toward that horizon
so that we, beholders of that shadow,
feel ourselves shudder for some reason.

The Harvest, Avully

We are old, but not so old,
Marco, his gray t-shirt with its NASA emblem,
Claude, his blue Ford tractor
out back of the shed, the timeless Rhône beyond.
A dozen storks circle us,
their pale bodies, wings outstretched.
We pop Pinot Noir handfuls
into our mouths, their juice staining our palms.
We've set out the paniers de vendange.
Beside the vineyard rows we chew fresh parsley.
We sample yellow tomatoes,
Marco reminding us that storks bring renewal.
In the petite farmhouse with lace curtains,
he sets out glasses sparkling with the cool pink liquid: rosé.
We are old, but not so old.
Somehow, the subject of the blues comes up.
I reach for my phone to snag B.B. King on iTunes.
Yes, I say everybody wanna know
Why I sing the blues.
Well, I've been around a long time,
I really have paid my dues.
Glasses are raised. *C'est le moment*
de la récolte, the harvest. *Il faut vivre*, one must live.

To the Dogs of Segesta, Sicily

Dogs are better than human beings
because they know but do not tell.
Emily Dickinson

Why do you sleep?
And what do you guard, curled
like question marks,

sandy brown,
your hind feet tucked
beneath soft chins?

Why do you sleep?
See how lazy you've become,
eyes mere black slits,

the trio of you
sprawled, ears drooping, white
underbellies exposed,

legs splayed
across the gravel walk. I dare to extend
an arm your way.

One of you, the pup, barely rouses
to sniff at my offered ham sandwich
and gobble it down

before shutting its eyes again.
Why do you pay no mind to us who come
to visit this ancient place?

Here the proud have fallen,
so many warriors of the Elymians, Greeks,
Romans, Normans,

the ancient city now rubble, here
after earthquakes, pestilence, war. You rest
among the vestiges.

Sneakered tourists
step over you. Tour guides
ignore where you lie.

Each night for two millennia
the constellations have risen over
Artemis's unfinished temple,

solid but empty now
up the path from where you lie, its rugged
stones against the dark sky.

Why do you sleep? The world
is a boiling cauldron. So has it ever been,
and so will it be.

In your dreams you are
hounds of Artemis. Your fangs drip red
as you tear the stag limb from limb.

In your dreams you roam
the night sky like mythical canines
changed by Dionysius into stars.

Farewell to Li Hao

You will make me tea
in your new embassy. You're *returning*, you say.
That means coming back, I think.

We survey the mountains of China
staring up to atrium murals of the Tien Shan,
Altay, Himalayas.

We walk under glass clouds,
a thousand little ones that hang from the skylight.
The cloud of fortune, you say.

In the side banquet room
our two chairs face toward the center
of vacant official space.

You pour out the tea,
the pot positioned exactly between us.
We absorb the silence.

It dawns on me that *returning* means
the going back to your own country, the center
of your known universe.

What do we need presidents for,
I ask, when we two could solve the tough problems
with just our own ideas?

Sipping, you glance into my eyes for just a second.
Big potatoes have their topics, you say. But as for us,
we have our duties.

We part by the guard station,
our diplomatic embrace watched from behind
through bulletproof glass.

Safety Information Card

Everything is planned for,
the story, koan-like,
in few words,
diagrams, hieroglyphics.
Becalmed passengers turn,
facial features unrecognizable,
to their tasks: the woman
directed by a brilliant
red arrow pulls dutifully
on the hatch handle
to open it without effort
to a danger-free world,
bereft of all angst.
A mother with placid eyes
cups an oxygen mask,
her own already in place,
to the face of a child,
a child who delights
in the bright yellow toy.
Words leap tri-lingually
telling what to do:
Si usted está sentado
en una fila de salida, . . .
Si vous êtes assiss
près d'une issue de secours, . . .
If you are seated
in the exit row, . . .
So little left to chance.
The aircraft noses its way,

ever tranquilly, downward
onto a pleasant ocean.
Orange seat cushions
rise by themselves
ever so easily into hands,
as travelers file onto
an intact wing
to cast themselves
into the gentle waves.
It is the best of beach days.
One simply pulls the life-vest cord
to float serenely to rescue.

To the Subjunctive

Big "what if," big unreality,
you contain our wishes, our possibilities:

were I three inches taller,
had I but world enough and time.

Dear mood, dear abstraction,
the dogwoods would have been in blossom,

and oh that the bills
had all been paid, the back porch painted!

Thank you for helping us to wish,
recommend, refer, request or insist.

If our imagination
runs away, you run right alongside,

you who hold all that we
could have, should have, would have, but didn't.

.

The Twenty

First there's the green of it, which isn't green
but black on a green background,
at least on the obverse.
And it isn't a note, but it calls itself a note,
and one might become carried away
by those mesh patterns
of its borders, the lady's fishnet stocking
feel to them, and then Jackson, hair
blown by a patriotic wind.
What makes him deserving of this tribute,
his scowl into the distance, mouth
stern, grimacing?
Then there's the White House, proud, symmetrical,
its leaf-fringed border, ocean green
on the greenback reverse.
Such a crisp thing, adorned as it is by so many eagles
whose talons clutch olive branches, clutch shields,
clutch arrows.

ACKNOWLEDGEMENT

I'm grateful to the editors of *Innisfree Poetry* and *Nth Position* in which some of these poems first appeared, and to poetry workshop leaders Indran Amirthanayagam, Richard Blanco, Gary Sange, Michele Wolf and the late Stanley Plumly for their guidance, as well as to Daniela Hernández Rodríguez for her advice on Spanish and, last but most important to poet Nany Allinson, my wife, for her companionship, love and inspiration.

MARTIN DICKINSON

Is the author of three previous collections of poems: *Life List Notes* (Sligo Creek, 2021); together with his wife, poet Nancy Allinson, *What a Windstorm Teaches* (Sligo Creek, 2019); and *My Concept of Time* (Finishing Line, 2014). He was poet of the month for May 2015 for the online journal *Blue Heron Review*. Dickinson's poems appear in *Beltway Poetry Quarterly, California Quarterly, Innisfree Poetry Journal*, the Russian language weekly *Kontinent* (in translation) and several other print and online journals. He and Nancy live in Friendship Heights, Washington, D.C.

I AM THAT ROAD

PRINTING WAS COMPLETED IN AUGUST 2025 FOR **Beltway Editions**